Look What the Animals Taught Me!

True Life Stories for Children

Written By: Barbara L. Finney

Edited By: Laura M. Williams

Copyright © 2013 by Barbara L. Finney and Laura M. Williams

Look What the Animals Taught Me!
True Life Stories for Children
by Barbara L. Finney and Laura M. Williams

Printed in the United States of America

ISBN 9781628391947

All rights reserved solely by the author. The author guarantees all contents are original and do not infringe upon the legal rights of any other person or work. No part of this book may be reproduced in any form without the permission of the author. The views expressed in this book are not necessarily those of the publisher.

Unless otherwise indicated, Bible quotations are taken from the King James Version of the Bible.

www.xulonpress.com

Table of Contents

Chapters	Verses	Page Numbers
I. The Red Cobra		6
God's Word	Psalm 37:23	
	Psalm 119:5, 9	
II. The Marching Ants		8
God's Love	Psalm 91:1-5a	
	John 3:16	
III. The Reappearing Snake		12
God's Son	Matthew 28:6	
	Ephesians 1:19-20	
IV. The Green Mamba		16
God's Way	Psalm 16:11	
	John 14:6	
V. The Lion		18
God's Enemy	I Peter 5:8-10	
	Ephesians 6:13	
VI. The Kingfisher		20
God's Lesson	Colossians 2:6	
	I John 1:9	
VII. The Elephant		22
God's Help	Psalm 34:4	
	Acts 16:31	
	I Thessalonians 5:17	
	James 5:16b	
VIII. The Genet Cat		26
God's Warning	Psalm 119:133	
	Romans 8:37	

The Red Cobra

God's Word

Suddenly, I was frozen where I stood! In the path was a red cobra! Oh, how I shouted for someone to come to my rescue as quickly as they could!

When I first arrived in Kenya, East Africa; I was told to bring a flashlight. The flashlight would be necessary at night when I was walking outside along the dark African pathways. I needed the light to help me find snakes and other deadly creatures that might threaten my safety.

There are many types of snakes in Kenya, but the most common in our area was the red cobra. The red colored snake seems to stand when it is ready to strike. This spitting cobra has fangs that forcefully eject a stream of venom or poison into its prey. There is a lot of pain and damage if the poison reaches the eyes. Many times the dogs suffered because of these cobras in the bush, causing them pain and loss of eyesight.

These snakes average from four to six feet in length and usually slither on the ground. Occasionally, they can be found high in the trees. Because of the possibility of a red cobra falling on me, I was constantly pointing my flashlight toward the trees and then to the ground and back again.

One night, I was returning to my little mud brick house from our evening prayer meeting. As I walked, I was singing and looking up into the trees. Suddenly, I had a sinking feeling in the pit of my stomach! The Lord was warning me about something! I quickly shone my light on the ground. To my horror, I saw my foot stepping over the tail of a red cobra! It was in a hurry to get away and I fled in the other direction! Running frantically, I called out for Marion, a fellow missionary with a gun.

As soon as she arrived, we began to cautiously hunt for the snake. The red cobra was hiding from us! Marion discovered the cobra in a striking position on the steps of my front porch! As I held my flashlight on the cobra, I could see just how huge this reptile really was. Marion took aim with a steady hand, and shot the creature right through the head.

That night I learned to keep my light focused on the path in front of me. God's Word can be a light in our daily walk. "O that my ways were directed to keep Thy statues!" Psalm 119:5. God's Word will reveal the right path. If we follow His path, we can avoid the dangers that come our way from any direction.

Psalm 119:9 clearly states, "Wherewithal shall a young man cleanse his way? by taking heed thereto according to Thy Word." We make many mistakes and commit many sins when our eyes and our steps do not follow the Light of God's Word. We may look to the world and fall into the path of temptation which we could have avoided. Psalm 37:23 helps us understand that, "The steps of a good man are ordered by the Lord: and he delighteth in his way." God's Word will give us light, as we travel in God's way.

Memory Verse…Psalm 119:9

The Marching Ants

God's Love

Watch out, Misty! The marching ants are trudging over your kittens! The kittens were being attacked by marching ants!

Africa is a very beautiful continent with numerous exotic creatures. One of these animals is a pain inflicting insect called the marching ant or army ant. It is much larger than the average ant and is black with long pinchers in the front of its body. Millions of these homeless ants walk together in long columns searching for food. They march on land, build bridges by crawling over one another, or float across streams using leaves as their boats. They form lines of two and sometimes four with guards posted on each side, going back and forth, ready to give a warning if enemies are found approaching.

They will quickly scatter, if a person steps in their pathway unexpectedly. Some will climb up the person's legs, intentionally waiting until several of their friends have climbed on and attached themselves to the skin, then they begin to bite. Their bite is very painful and they inject a small amount of poison. To a person it causes swelling and discomfort, but for a small animal like baby chicks or kittens, the bites can be deadly.

When the ants begin to march, it seems that nothing can stop their plan or their place of attack. If they are disturbed, they will reorganize and continue marching. If a house is in the middle of their path, they will go through the building. If the ants are frightened or redirected, they will scatter and fill that area. It is best to ignore the Army Ants and allow them to continue on their way.

Early one morning, I was awakened by loud desperate crying. The sound was coming from the front porch. My cat Misty and her four new kittens alerted me of danger. There was no electricity at that time, so I grabbed my flashlight to see why she was crying. I did not get very far when I found those huge black ants crawling up my pajamas legs.

When I got to the porch, I could see that the ants were attacking the new little kittens. Misty was trying to help, but those insects were everywhere! I began jumping frantically from place to place trying to step where the ants were not. When I reached the kittens, I picked them up, ants and all, and put them in the living room where I removed as many of the ants as I could. At the same time, I was pulling the biting ants off my own body!

I took the kittens one by one into the bathroom and put them in water to try to remove the ants that were still clinging to their small bodies. I gave the wet kittens to Misty so she could comfort them after I finished. This took quite a while and almost every room in my house had ants angrily crawling around. The only safe place was in my bed. So Misty and I, with the four kittens, got into my bed to rest from our battle. By morning, all the kittens were fine and the ants had continued on their way, carrying most of the dead ants with them.

I was greatly impressed with the love of the mother cat, risking her life while trying to save her babies. She had no defense against so many ants and yet, there she was in the middle of the danger, running from kitten to kitten trying to help.

It made me think of God`s love for us, which is greater than any love! He did not risk His life; He gave His life for us. There is no greater love!

Unlike Misty, God is able to protect us from any danger. We can rest in the arms of the Heavenly Father. Are you safe in the arms of Jesus as your Savior?

"He that dwelleth in the secret place of the Most High shall abide under the shadow of the Almighty. I will say of the Lord, He is my refuge and my fortress: my God; in Him will I trust. Surely He shall deliver thee from the snare of the fowler, and from the noisome pestilence. He shall cover thee with His feathers, and under His wings shalt thou trust: His truth shall be thy shield and buckler. Thou shalt not be afraid…" (Ps. 91:1-5a)

God`s love and protection for His children is far greater than we can imagine. One of the most familiar verses, John 3:16, tells us that God so loved us that He sacrificed His only begotten Son for us! How can man, woman, boy, or girl reject so great a love as this?

Memory Verse…Psalm 91:2

The Reappearing Snake

God's Son

Ahh! I thought that puff adder was dead! It was moving straight toward me!

During the rainy season, the grass grows very quickly, really high, and extremely thick. A person has to be very watchful of snakes hiding in the tall grass. One such deadly snake is the puff adder. Its short, round, spongy body is grayish and very slow moving. This reptile is hard to spot because it is only about two feet long and very good at hiding. The puff adder kills more humans in Africa that any other snake; therefore people fear these lethal reptiles.

One day Mumo, an African worker, was cutting the tall, thick grass near the fence at the back of my house. He was using a grass slasher which is a long, thin, sharp metal blade which is curved on the end. Mumo was swinging the slasher in a rhythmic motion cutting the grass inch by inch. Suddenly he noticed that the area had become very quiet. Kenyans know that silence could mean the birds had sensed a snake nearby. All was eerily quiet. Noiselessly and very gradually, Mumo began to look all around. Lifting his bare feet gently in the tall grass, the worker saw two large puff adders! Using his grass cutter and a big stick, Mumo struck both of them with a mighty blow. Making sure they were dead, he brought them to my front yard. We took pictures and measured to see just how big these snakes actually were. When we finished, Mumo took the lifeless bodies and threw them far away.

About six o'clock the next evening, I was called to return to the hospital to see a patient. It was Sunday and my turn to be on duty. Since it was still light outside, I did not take my flashlight. By the time I headed home, it was almost dark. I met some of my missionary friends going to church for the evening service and they offered to let me borrow one of their flashlights. I thanked them, but thought I could make it safely home before dark.

As I neared my house, it was very dark and I could just barely make out the form of a snake in the pathway! As I got closer, I could see it was a puff adder! I thought someone must have played a trick on me. Mumo had just killed that snake yesterday. This was the same place I had taken pictures of the dead snakes! Wait! I thought I saw it move! I started screaming, "Help! Snake!" No one was around. I picked up a stick, but it was too short! I ran to my porch for a broom, but it was not heavy enough!

I was determined not to lose sight of that snake, so I quickly called the hospital and a young lady on night duty tried to find someone to come out while I rushed back outside to watch the snake. This time I brought my flashlight. The puff adder had not moved far when I returned. Another missionary named Gary arrived with a panga, which is a very long knife. He killed the snake and we both laughed about my thoughts of the snake coming back to life again.

This story made me think of the only One Who died and rose again. According to Matthew 28:6 the angel encouraged the ladies at the tomb not to be afraid, "He is not here: for He is risen, as He said. Come, see the place where the Lord lay."

Yes, Jesus died, but as the Word of God and many witnesses tell us, death could not hold Him. He arose from the dead so that everyone may have eternal life, if they will simply receive Him as their Savior.

"And what is the exceeding greatness of His power to us-ward who believe, according to the working of His mighty power, which He wrought in Christ, when He raised Him from the dead, and set Him at His own right hand in the heavenly places." Ephesians 1:19-20.

Memory Verse…Matthew 28:6

The Green Mamba

God's Way

I went the wrong way! I discovered that I was hiding in a room with a poisonous snake! "Lord, please keep me safe!" I prayed fervently.

The African people fear another snake called the green mamba. Though they are not as aggressive as their relatives, the black mambas, they are still deadly. Living mostly in the trees, mambas are poisonous snakes that can kill a human who is bitten in only fifteen minutes.

After the morning roll call followed by devotions with our African nurses, we began to go to our different departments. Our little hospital, located in Mwingi in the middle of a dry bushy area, is divided into several different buildings. The nursing unit, where my group was headed, was on top of a hill. As we were making our way up the hill, a lady shouted, "Snake!"

Everyone scattered! Our doctor arrived and he called to an older man who worked at the hospital, "Maithya, where is the snake?"

There was a man standing beside Maithya. He was holding a stick about six feet long. He said, "I don't know, this woman saw the snake."

"Yes, yes," The woman spoke excitedly in Kikamba, her tribal language, "It was a green one, the bad kind, and it ran under that door."

The lady was pointing in my direction! That door was the entrance to the room I had gone through to escape. Everyone got a stick and began searching as I quickly ducked into another room to hide. I knew how dangerous this snake's bite would be if he found me. Suddenly the lady shouted, "Not that room!" She turned and to my horror, pointed in my direction again, "The snake is in there!" My heart leaped and sank all at the same time! I scurried out of the room as fast as I could!

The men began beating their sticks all around the room, trying to drive the snake from its hiding place. Then there was a loud shout, "Look! Up there!"

Crawling along the rafters in the ceiling was the green mamba. The snake was probably laughing at us as we jumped around. Later the men were able to chase it down and kill it.

The lady chose the wrong room because she did not know which way the snake had gone. I chose the wrong way because I was in the room with the snake. Have you made wrong choices in your life? Have you gone the wrong way? What path have you chosen to follow? God's promises are true and show us the right way if we will obey.

"Thou wilt shew me the path of life: in Thy presence is fullness of joy; at Thy right hand are pleasures for evermore." Psalm 16:11.

God's way should be the way we choose every time. In John 14:6 Jesus said, "I am the way, the truth, and the life: no man cometh unto the Father, but by me." There is no other way to Heaven, but Jesus. If you are trying another way, you are lost. Jesus is pointing sinners in the right direction. Remember, it is not by my works of righteousness which I have done, but according to His grace.

Memory Verse… John 14:6

The Lion

God's Enemy

The lion stared at us, two frightened tourists! I thought he was going to attack my car! We were in his territory and perhaps he would make us his dinner!

Lions in Kenya are not as plentiful today as they have been in years past; however, some of these fierce mammals can be found in the game parks, weighing over 500 pounds. The police on the game reserves feed them meat to keep them from leaving the game parks. The lions are free to wander; they are not fenced in. There are signs warning of the danger all over the game parks.

One day, I was on a picture safari with another missionary. The guide warned us to be aware of all the wildlife. We saw several land rovers driving through and around the bushes. I was driving and it was difficult to see into the underbrush. As we came around one clump of bushes, there sat a beautiful lioness. The land rovers in front of my little Volkswagen began to stop and take pictures. Jane, the other missionary, was in the back seat. She was very anxious to snap a nice clear picture. She persuaded me to drive a little closer. As I edged my car closer, we were amazed to see a very large male lion sitting with his powerful paws crossed. His face was fierce, and yet handsome.

"What a wonderful picture that will make!" Jane exclaimed as we stopped the car. She was so excited that she thrust her camera and her head out the window! The lion did not like his privacy invaded by a couple of nosy sightseers. He suddenly came to a half-springing position and let out a frightening roar. We both jumped and she rapidly jerked her head and camera back into the car. We swiftly rolled up the windows as the lion began to slowly move our way. Then, just as suddenly, both lions turned and bolted into the bush. This was the closest encounter I had ever had with a lion.

The Bible says in I Peter 5:8 that Satan is like a roaring lion, seeking who he can devour. Devour means to eat greedily. We must be just as careful of Satan as we would be of a real lion. We cannot make Satan our friend, He is our adversary or our enemy and his aim is to destroy us no matter how handsome or lovely he appears. God is our Friend. He loves us and wants to protect us from our dangerous enemy. God loves us so much that He gave us His Word that we might know about the love of Jesus and the plan He has so carefully designed for each of our lives.

We are not physically strong enough to defeat a real lion or fast enough to run away either. Just as we are not strong enough to resist God`s enemy on our own. But God says if we resist steadfastly in the faith and look to God for our strength, He will, because of Jesus, make you stronger and give you the victory. (I Peter 5:9-10)

Memory Verse…Ephesians 6:13

The Kingfisher

God's Lesson

Watch out, Mr. Kingfisher! Please don't play in the wet cement! Jon, help the beautiful bird escape! Hurry, time is running out!

The kingfisher is a beautiful red and blue colored African bird. This small colorful bird has a large head, a long sharp pointed bill, short legs, and a stubby tail. The kingfisher preys mainly on insects.

There was a kingfisher seen flying playfully around the mission's water tanks. Every morning he would sit in a tree near my house. The lovely bird would flutter from limb to limb, and then fly to the ground. Mr. Kingfisher appeared very proud as if he wanted to show off his beauty. Each morning I awoke, looked out my window, and there he would be showing off his vibrantly colored feathers.

The workmen were building a new water tank near my house. They would dig a hole for water; then dip the bricks in the water before cementing them. Mr. Kingfisher was a very inquisitive or curious bird. He would fly around observing all the activity. Often, he would fly dangerously close to the water hole.

One day as Gary, another missionary and his son Jon, were watching the work, they noticed my lively friend. They watched Mr. Kingfisher fly much too close to the water which was thick with sand and cement. His curiosity allowed him to get trapped in the wet cement. By the time Jon had rescued him, the frightened little bird had almost drowned. They dried him off and put him in the nice warm sun. As soon as he recovered, Mr. Kingfisher was flying happily from branch to branch again.

The next morning I looked for my beautiful friend, but he was not there to greet me as he had done the days before. I found that Mr. Kingfisher had again flown too close to the wet cement, but this time no one was around to save him. Unfortunately, Mr. Kingfisher did not learn from his mistake.

Do we make the same mistakes over and over again? When we make mistakes or do wrong things, the Lord warns us about our sin. We must listen to God and His Word when we are cautioned to beware of sin in our lives. Jesus wants us to pray and seek His help and forgiveness when we are doing wrong. Jesus has shown us examples in His Word of how we must stay close to Him. We should not stray, or go back to our old ways, for if we do we will fall into the same trouble. We can have joy and strength in our Christian walk when we take heed to the warnings and obey. Colossians 2:6 encourages us, "As you have therefore received Christ Jesus the Lord, so walk ye in Him."

Memory Verse...I John 1:9

The Elephant

God's Help

My car was dying, Jane was nervous, and there were wild animal all around! I prayed, "Lord, please help that elephant to move over! How will You deliver us out of this one?"

Most people think of Africa as a jungle, but Kenya has many hills and trees along with the wildlife too. The capital city is Nairobi. Many tourists who visit Kenya enjoy going to the game parks to see all the wild animals outside the capital. There are gravel roads and no fences throughout the game parks. Tsavo, one of the largest parks, is well known for its many elephants.

Jane, a missionary friend, and I took a few days away from our work at the Mwingi Hospital. We decided to go on a picture-shooting safari. As we drove into the reserve outside Nairobi, almost immediately we saw a huge, dusty, brown elephant. The tourists all drove around him taking pictures from different angles because he did not seem to mind. We were told later by the park rangers that if an elephant becomes frightened or upset, he may charge your car. They warned us to be careful because these animals are wild!

We spent the day driving all around the reserve taking some magnificent pictures. We saw gazelles, hartebeests, zebras, giraffes, warthogs, and many elephants. There was a place near the road where we saw a herd of elephants just standing there. I put the little Volkswagen bug in neutral and aimed my camera at the group. The oldest looking elephant began to flap his ears and lift his long powerful trunk. I could read his thoughts immediately and I knew I had better get out of there as fast as I could! I threw down my camera and put the car into reverse. Suddenly I realized that the motor had shut off without any warning! I looked back at the angry elephant to see his reaction. Miraculously the elephant stopped! Praise the Lord! With my palms sweaty and shaking, I tried to restart my car. This time the motor roared to life and I quickly left the elephants to frighten someone else.

The next morning, Jane and I drove to Mzima Springs to the see the hippos. There were three large ones playing in the water. We lost track of time as we watched and enjoyed the hippos playing their games. It was getting late and the park rules stated that you must be in your cabin by six o'clock. We quickly left to return to our cabin when we realized how late it was. In our hurry, we took the wrong road. It was already six o'clock by the time we realized our mistake. The darkness was quickly closing in and all the animals seemed to lose their fear of humans as they wandered around freely.

I was speeding along, when I noticed a huge form ahead of us in the middle of the road! As we came closer, I could see a gigantic elephant in our way! I was sure that if I honked, it would only make him angry. I cautiously followed his slow moving steps from a safe distance behind. I was hoping he would eventually move over, but he did not! Jane and I discussed whether it would be a good idea to start up really fast, honk, and try to pass him. All I could see in my mind was a giant foot stepping on my car and flattening us!

For close to an hour, the giant elephant would take a step, swing his trunk to one side, and stand there awhile. My car was starting to overheat because of the extremely slow pace. I was really concerned that my car was not going to make it. We decided to stop and pray for him to MOVE OVER! We were not able to go anywhere until God moved him out of our way. As we prayed and waited, the sky was growing darker by the minute and my gas was getting low. My last hope was that the rangers would find us before we became dinner for some hungry animal.

Suddenly the elephant began to very slowly move over. When I was sure that there was just enough room, I made my move! Holding my breath, I stepped on the gas and sped around him. I was so thankful to be back in the cabin that night!

Are there any objects in your life that need to be moved or removed? You may have problems or sins which seem too big for you to move. God is able to take care of moving that sin or problem. The Bible says in James 5:16b, "The effectual fervent prayer of a righteous man availeth much." First Thessalonians 5:17 states, "Pray without ceasing." The Lord is faithful and He can help you as well as keep you from evil. He can remove anything that is in our way and teaching us to trust Him as He does. God is able to do more than you ever thought possible, but you have to trust Him.

If you are not a child of the King, He is waiting for you to confess your sin and ask Him to save you from your sin. He can cleanse you from all unrighteousness. Acts 16:31 says, "Believe on the Lord Jesus Christ, and thou shalt be saved, and thy house."

Memory Verse… Psalm 34:4

The Genet Cat

God's Warning

I did not invite him! The dogs were trying to jump through my screen door to save me! My neighbor's son ran to get his gun!

Genet cats are small animals, usually a dark color mixed with white. Their name means small bear. Genet cats are more closely related to the mongoose than to the cat family. Their tails are as long as their bodies and whatever their head can fit though, so can their bodies. Genets are very agile creatures, good at climbing, jumping, and running. They can also be very cruel animals in the wild.

In Kenya, the summer can be extremely hot. On this particular day, the sun was blazing in the bright blue sky. I was a missionary nurse who helped people when they were sick. My favorite part of being a missionary was when I got to share the gospel with the people and help then grow in the Lord and His Word.

I had returned to my home from our little mud brick clinic for a cool drink and some lunch. I was very tired from a combination of hard work and the extreme heat. It was much cooler in the house, so I decided to take a short nap after lunch.

As I slept, Jon, a neighboring missionary's son, came over to borrow some ice from my refrigerator. The ten year old froze when he saw a genet cat sitting on a table in my house. Suddenly he raced back toward his house, slamming the door on his way to get his B. B. gun and call for help.

That noise from my porch woke me up! People were screaming, dogs were barking, and doors were banging! I jumped out of my bed and ran to see what was happening. To my horror in the next room, in the middle of my round blue table sat a genet cat. During all this commotion, our German Shepherd dogs were trying to jump through the screen door to come to my rescue.

The genet understood that he was not welcome. These animals are very dangerous, so we had to be very careful. Jon returned with his gun, took careful aim, and… before he could shoot, the genet took off. He climbed up the screen and got between the screen and the tin roof. He squeezed out and headed for the barbed wire fence. The dogs were too quick for the intruder and caught him. The genet was trapped and after a few minutes of snarling and snapping he was killed. So much for my peaceful lunch hour, it was time to return to the clinic.

As Christians, we should be careful of the unwelcome sins in our lives. They will come in as tiny sins, but can easily grow too large to handle before we realize it. Sin can cause all sorts of troubles, leaving us with many sorrows and scars to deal with for the rest of our lives. God gives us warnings concerning these intruders. Psalm 119:133 says, "Order my steps in thy Word: and let not any iniquity have dominion over me." No sin can overtake us if we allow God to direct us through His quick and powerful Word. The Holy Spirit will then guide us as we hide God's Word in our hearts so that we will not sin against the Lord.

Memory Verse… Romans 8:37

Conclusion

I.	God's Word	Are you memorizing God's Word?
II.	God's Love	Do you know God's love?
III.	God's Son	Have you trusted God's Son as your Savior?
IV.	God's Way	Have you chosen God's way?
V.	God's Enemy	Are you ready to stand against God's enemy?
VI.	God's Lessons	Do you understand God's lessons?
VII.	God's Help	Are you asking for God's help?
VIII.	God's Warnings	Do you listen to God's warnings?

CPSIA information can be obtained at www.ICGtesting.com
Printed in the USA
LVOW02s0500071214

417593LV00001B/1/P